For little Laurence – *R.R.*

For all my sisters – *Z.H.*

Magination Press

Books for Kids From the
American Psychological Association

First published in 2021 by Andersen Press Ltd. Original version text copyright © 2021 Rachel Rooney, illustrations copyright © 2021 Zehra Hicks.

Magination Press is a registered trademark of the American Psychological Association.

Order books at maginationpress.org, or call 1-800-374-2721.

Cataloguing-in-Publication is available at the Library of Congress.

ISBN: 978-1-4338-4195-8

Printed in China

10 9 8 7 6 5 4 3 2 1

The Worrying WORRIES

BY RACHEL ROONEY   ILLUSTRATED BY ZEHRA HICKS

MAGINATION PRESS · AMERICAN PSYCHOLOGICAL ASSOCIATION · WASHINGTON, D.C.

Once, I found a Worry so I trapped it in a net.

I picked it out and put it in my pocket for a pet.

Everywhere I went that day, my Worry came with me.

The library...

the stores...

the park...

and home again at three.

It soon became a nuisance.

It tangled up my hair.

It tugged my sleeve.

It itched my skin.

It stole my favorite chair.

I pushed away my pasta.

I couldn't eat my cake.

I lost my appetite
because I'd got a
stomach ache.

But Worries have a hunger.
They feed upon your fears.

It nibbled on my
fingernails...

and sipped my salty tears.

It whispered mean words in my ear.

Put sad thoughts in my head.

It followed me upstairs...

... and hogged the covers on my bed.

It fidgeted and wiggled.

It met me in my sleep.

When I woke I knew it was a pet I couldn't keep.

I'd had enough of worrying.
I took my Worry pet
to see a Worry Expert.
(She was once a Worry Vet.)

I told her what the matter was.
She nodded once or twice.
She rubbed her chin and thought a bit.
Then offered this advice...

A Worry is an awful pest but it won't do you harm.
Try these simple exercises. They will keep you calm.

We practiced
painting pictures in
our head.
We shut our eyes.
And thought of

sunshine...

beaches...

flowers...

ice cream...

butterflies.

We practiced statue-standing.

Kept as still as we could be.

Breathing slowly in and out while counting...

One...

Two...

Three.

We practiced squeezing muscles tighter than a mother's hug.

Then made our bodies floppy like a jelly or a slug.

Keep practicing, the expert said.
Your day has just begun.

Now you need to leave and
practice having lots of fun...

I followed her instructions...

It seemed to do the trick.

I haven't seen the Worry since.

Now I'm not worried sick.

Reader's Note
by Tammy L. Hughes, PhD

Reading *The Worrying Worries* can help children to identify and manage their experiences of worry. Helping children to identify and sort thoughts like worry (which happen in your mind), feelings (which happen in your body), and actions (things you do) helps them to develop early awareness about themselves and others. As children age, this is a book that can be revisited to illustrate how the mind and body are connected and how their thinking can impact or change how they interpret their feelings. As children mature, they develop the ability to control their behavior by regulating their thoughts and feelings. This book provides a lighthearted way to start these discussions with young minds.

What Is Worry?

Fear is a basic emotion we are a born with, a response to danger. It is unvoluntary. In contrast, worry is a *thought* that something bad might happen. Unlike an emotion we are born with, worry is manufactured. Worry becomes connected to fear when thoughts center on future potential dangers.

Children often pick up worries from the adults around them. Children will copy the models they see or take up worries they overhear or observe in the grown-ups around them. Parents and caregivers can help by modeling healthy ways of coping with worries.

Recognizing and Managing Worry

It is common to believe that worry helps us to prepare for possible negative life events and to find the best solutions, even though it usually doesn't. If events do turn out well, this strengthens the belief that bracing ourselves with worry was worth it. Ironically, if events turn out poorly, we are quicker to experience unhelpful thoughts since we were already on that path with worry. This cycle can lead to chronic worrying. In the book, when worry starts to whisper and become bigger and bigger, the narrator notices something needs to be done to change things. Point out how the child both notices their worry is too much and then decides to act. Not only does this stop a cycle from developing, but it also promotes self-determination and feelings of accomplishment.

The following are some strategies for managing worries.

Distraction

The book illustrates useful examples of distraction. Mindfulness techniques, such as deep breathing, meditation, and yoga poses, promote a focus on the here and now and away from anticipating problems. Reading, arts and crafts, watching movies, playing games and other activities where they tend to be absorbed or in a state of flow (intense and focused concentration) can be positive distractions.

Validation

Listen to your child's concerns and reassure them that their worries are normal. Children often like to hear that many kids their age think about the same things. Let them know you understand. It is not helpful to contradict them. Saying "There's nothing to worry about" can make kids conclude that they shouldn't feel the way they do, or worse, make them less likely to share again. Rather, validating how they feel keeps the conversation going.

Refocusing on The Positives

Start by asking your child to name three things each day that worked out well for them. Then ask them to name three things that worked out well for someone else. Once you are into the habit of noticing positives, ask your child what they *did* to make things work out well, or what someone else *did* to make things work out well for themselves. Some kids have a hard time noticing their own efforts, so focusing on others makes it easier to observe cause and effect. As your child begins to see how their own efforts result in desired outcomes, worries tend to recede. To get this started, you can tell your child about the good things that happened for you and what you did to cause them. It is okay to talk about worries, but it helps to focus on the good moments and where they have the opportunity to influence the outcome.

Like feelings, thoughts can come and go. Teaching children to acknowledge thoughts, without overly attending to them, is helpful to them. Thoughts are a critical part of mental health and wellness. Children benefit from exposure to how they work. When thoughts are persistent and disruptive to the child then it may be time to check with a mental health care professional.

Tammy L. Hughes, PhD, ABPP is a school psychologist, licensed psychologist and board certified in school psychology, and a professor at Duquesne University in Pittsburgh, PA.